MW00379190

Presented to

On the occasion of

From

Date

SELECTIONS FROM

THE BIBLE PROMISE BOOK

BARBOUR
PUBLISHING, INC.

ISBN 1-57748-719-2

All Scripture is from the King James Version of the Bible.

Published by Barbour Publishing, Inc., P.O. Box 719, Uhrichsville, Ohio 44683
http://www.barbourbooks.com

Printed in China.

Introduction

Whatever the need of the moment, the answer is to be found in Scripture, if we take the time to search for it. Whatever we're feeling, whatever we're suffering, whatever we're hoping, the Bible has something to say to us.

This collection of Bible verses, in a beautiful gift book format, is meant to encourage you when you need the Bible's guidance for a particular area of your life. It is in no way intended to replace regular Bible study or the use of a concordance for in-depth study of a subject. There are many facets of your life and many topics in the Bible that are not covered here.

But if, for example, you are feeling extremely lonely one day, some of the Bible's wisdom and comfort is available to you here under the topic of Loneliness. All topics are arranged alphabetically, for ease of use, and all Scripture is from the King James Version of the Bible.

In addition to the encouragement of the Scriptures, this package features a compact disc of praise and worship music, to enhance your devotional experience.

Contents

BELIEF

For God so loved the world, that he gave his only begotten Son,
that whosoever believeth in him should not perish,
but have everlasting life.
John 3:16

To him give all the prophets witness,
that through his name whosoever believeth in him
shall receive remission of sins.
Acts 10:43

As it is written, Behold, I lay in Sion a stumblingstone and rock of offence: and whosoever believeth on him shall not be ashamed.
Romans 9:33

But as many as received him, to them gave he power to become the sons of God, even to them that believe on his name.
John 1:12

He that believeth on him is not condemned: but he that believeth not is condemned already, because he hath not believed in the name of the only begotten Son of God.
John 3:18

He that believeth on the Son hath everlasting life: and he that believeth not the Son shall not see life; but the wrath of God abideth on him.
John 3:36

Charity

Blessed is he that considereth the poor:
the LORD will deliver him in time of trouble.
The LORD will preserve him, and keep him alive;
and he shall be blessed upon the earth:
and thou wilt not deliver him unto the will of his enemies.
Psalm 41:1–2

He that hath pity upon the poor lendeth unto the LORD;
and that which he hath given will he pay him again.
Proverbs 19:17

But when thou makest a feast, call the poor, the maimed,
the lame, the blind: And thou shalt be blessed;
for they cannot recompense thee: for thou shalt be recompensed
at the resurrection of the just.
Luke 14:13–14

Sell that ye have, and give alms; provide yourselves bags
which wax not old, a treasure in the heavens that faileth not,
where no thief approacheth, neither moth corrupteth.
Luke 12:33

He that despiseth his neighbour sinneth:
but he that hath mercy on the poor, happy is he.
Proverbs 14:21

Comfort

God is our refuge and strength,
a very present help in trouble.
Therefore will not we fear,
though the earth be removed,
and though the mountains
be carried into the midst of the sea;
Though the waters thereof roar
and be troubled,
though the mountains
shake with the swelling thereof.

Psalm 46:1–3

Though I walk in the midst of trouble, thou wilt revive me:
thou shalt stretch forth thine hand against the wrath of mine enemies,
and thy right hand shall save me.
Psalm 138:7

Though he fall, he shall not be utterly cast down:
for the LORD upholdeth him with his hand.
Psalm 37:24

The LORD is my rock, and my fortress, and my deliverer;
my God, my strength, in whom I will trust;
my buckler, and the horn of my salvation, and my high tower.
Psalm 18:2

For he hath not despised nor abhorred the affliction
of the afflicted; neither hath he hid his face from him;
but when he cried unto him, he heard.
Psalm 22:24

Contentment

A merry heart doeth good like a medicine:
but a broken spirit drieth the bones.
Proverbs 17:22

Let your conversation be without covetousness;
and be content with such things as ye have: for he hath said,
I will never leave thee, nor forsake thee.
Hebrews 13:5

All the days of the afflicted are evil:
but he that is of a merry heart
hath a continual feast.
Proverbs 15:15

A sound heart is the life of the flesh:
but envy the rottenness of the bones.
Proverbs 14:30

But godliness with contentment is great gain.
1 Timothy 6:6

Let not thine heart envy sinners:
but be thou in the fear of the LORD all the day long.
For surely there is an end; and thine expectation
shall not be cut off.
Proverbs 23:17–18

God's Correction

For whom the Lord loveth he correcteth;
even as a father the son in whom he delighteth.
Proverbs 3:12

Behold, happy is the man whom God correcteth:
therefore despise not thou the chastening of the Almighty:
For he maketh sore, and bindeth up: he woundeth,
and his hands make whole.
Job 5:17–18

Blessed is the man whom thou chastenest, O LORD,
and teachest him out of thy law;
That thou mayest give him rest from the days of adversity,
until the pit be digged for the wicked.
Psalm 94:12–13

For which cause we faint not; but though our outward man perish,
yet the inward man is renewed day by day.
For our light affliction, which is but for a moment, worketh
for us a far more exceeding and eternal weight of glory.
2 Corinthians 4:16–17

For they verily for a few days chastened us after their own pleasure;
but he for our profit, that we might be partakers of his holiness.
Now no chastening for the present seemeth to be joyous,
but grievous: nevertheless afterward it yieldeth the peaceable fruit
of righteousness unto them which are exercised thereby.
Hebrews 12:10–11

COURAGE

Wait on the LORD:
be of good courage,
and he shall strengthen thine
heart: wait, I say, on the LORD.
Psalm 27:14

For the LORD loveth judgment,
and forsaketh not his saints;
they are preserved for ever:
but the seed of the wicked
shall be cut off.
Psalm 37:28

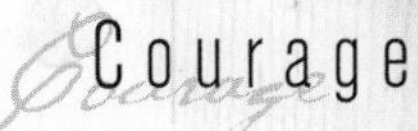

But now thus saith the LORD that created thee, O Jacob,
and he that formed thee, O Israel, Fear not: for I have redeemed thee,
I have called thee by thy name; thou art mine.
Isaiah 43:1

Fear not: for they that be with us are more
than they that be with them.
2 Kings 6:16

Trust in the LORD, and do good; so shalt thou dwell in the land,
and verily thou shalt be fed.
Psalm 37:3

He giveth power to the faint;
and to them that have no might he increaseth strength.
Isaiah 40:29

Eternal Life

Verily, verily, I say unto you,
He that believeth on me hath everlasting life.
John 6:47

Jesus said unto her, I am the resurrection, and the life:
he that believeth in me, though he were dead, yet shall he live:
And whosoever liveth and believeth in me shall never die.
Believest thou this?
John 11:25–26

Behold, I show you a mystery; We shall not all sleep,
but we shall all be changed,
In a moment, in the twinkling of an eye, at the last trump:
for the trumpet shall sound, and the dead shall
be raised incorruptible, and we shall be changed.
For this corruptible must put on incorruption,
and this mortal must put on immortality.
So when this corruptible shall have put on incorruption,
and this mortal shall have put on immortality, then shall be brought to
pass the saying that is written, Death is swallowed up in victory.
1 Corinthians 15:51–54

And this is the promise that he hath promised us, even eternal life.
1 John 2:25

For the Lord himself shall descend from heaven with a shout,
with the voice of the archangel, and with the trump of God:
and the dead in Christ shall rise first.
1 Thessalonians 4:16

Faith

Now faith is the substance of things hoped for,
the evidence of things not seen.
Hebrews 11:1

Watch ye, stand fast in the faith, quit you like men, be strong.
1 Corinthians 16:13

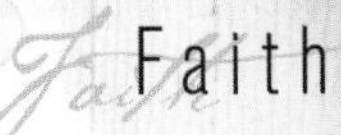

If any of you lack wisdom, let him ask of God, that giveth
to all men liberally, and upbraideth not; and it shall be given him.
But let him ask in faith, nothing wavering.
For he that wavereth is like a wave of the sea driven
with the wind and tossed.
James 1:5–6

For by grace are ye saved through faith;
and that not of yourselves: it is the gift of God.
Ephesians 2:8

For ye are all the children of God by faith in Christ Jesus.
Galatians 3:26

The fruit of the Spirit is love, joy, peace, longsuffering, gentleness,
goodness, faith, Meekness, temperance:
against such there is no law.
Galatians 5:22–23

God's Faithfulness

Know therefore that the Lord thy God, he is God,
the faithful God, which keepeth covenant and mercy with them
that love him and keep his commandments to a thousand generations.
Deuteronomy 7:9

(For the Lord thy God
is a merciful God;)
he will not forsake thee,
neither destroy thee,
nor forget the covenant
of thy fathers
which he sware
unto them.
Deuteronomy 4:31

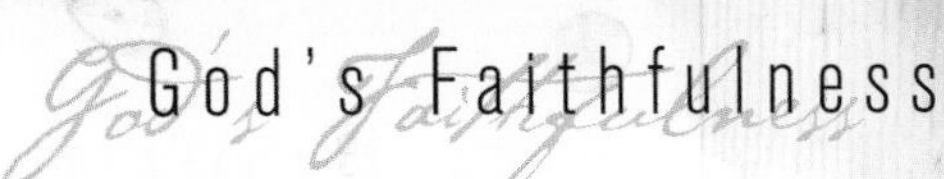

He hath remembered his covenant for ever, the word which he commanded to a thousand generations.
Psalm 105:8

God is not a man, that he should lie; neither the son of man, that he should repent: hath he said, and shall he not do it? or hath he spoken, and shall he not make it good?
Numbers 23:19

Let us hold fast the profession of our faith without wavering; (for he is faithful that promised).
Hebrews 10:23

The Lord is not slack concerning his promise, as some men count slackness; but is longsuffering to us-ward.
2 Peter 3:9

FORGIVENESS

But I say unto you, Love your enemies,
bless them that curse you, do good to them that hate you,
and pray for them which despitefully use you, and persecute you;
That ye may be the children of your Father which is in heaven:
for he maketh his sun to rise on the evil and on the good,
and sendeth rain on the just and on the unjust.
Matthew 5:44–45

For if ye forgive men their trespasses,
your heavenly Father will also forgive you.
Matthew 6:14

*Therefore if thine enemy hunger, feed him;
if he thirst, give him drink.*
Romans 12:20

But love ye your enemies, and do good, and lend,
hoping for nothing again; and your reward shall be great,
and ye shall be the children of the Highest:
for he is kind unto the unthankful and to the evil.
Be ye therefore merciful, as your Father also is merciful.
Judge not, and ye shall not be judged: condemn not,
and ye shall not be condemned: forgive,
and ye shall be forgiven.
Luke 6:35–37

FRUITFULNESS

And he shall be like a tree planted by the rivers of water,
that bringeth forth his fruit in his season; his leaf also shall not wither;
and whatsoever he doeth shall prosper.
Psalm 1:3

Therefore they shall come and sing in the height of Zion,
and shall flow together to the goodness of the LORD,
for wheat, and for wine, and for oil,
and for the young of the flock and of the herd:
and their soul shall be as a watered garden;
and they shall not sorrow any more at all.
Jeremiah 31:12

They shall still bring forth fruit in old age;
they shall be fat and flourishing.
Psalm 92:14

I will be as the dew unto Israel: he shall grow as the lily,
and cast forth his roots as Lebanon.
Hosea 14:5

Growth in Grace

Herein is my Father glorified,
that ye bear much fruit;
so shall ye be my disciples.
John 15:8

And this I pray,
that your love may abound
yet more and more in knowledge
and in all judgment.
Philippians 1:9

Being filled with the fruits of righteousness,
which are by Jesus Christ,
unto the glory and praise of God.
Philippians 1:11

But we all, with open face beholding as in a glass
the glory of the Lord, are changed into the same image
from glory to glory, even as by the Spirit of the Lord.
2 Corinthians 3:18

The LORD will perfect that which concerneth me: thy mercy,
O LORD, endureth for ever: forsake not the works of thine own hands.
Psalm 138:8

But the path of the just is as the shining light,
that shineth more and more unto the perfect day.
Proverbs 4:18

GUIDANCE

And thine ears shall hear a word behind thee, saying,
This is the way, walk ye in it, when ye turn to the right hand,
and when ye turn to the left.
Isaiah 30:21

For this God is our God for ever and ever:
he will be our guide even unto death.
Psalm 48:14

A man's heart deviseth his way: but the LORD directeth his steps.
Proverbs 16:9

The steps of a good man
are ordered by the LORD:
and he delighteth in his way.
Psalm 37:23

For his God doth instruct him to discretion, and doth teach him.
Isaiah 28:26

HELP IN TROUBLES

But the salvation of the righteous is of the LORD:
he is their strength in the time of trouble.
Psalm 37:39

The LORD openeth the eyes of the blind:
the LORD raiseth them that are bowed down:
the LORD loveth the righteous.
Psalm 146:8

The LORD is good, a strong hold in the day of trouble;
and he knoweth them that trust in him.
Nahum 1:7

Though he fall, he shall not be utterly cast down:
for the LORD upholdeth him with his hand.
Psalm 37:24

Thou art my hiding place; thou shalt preserve me from trouble;
thou shalt compass me about with songs of deliverance.
Psalm 32:7

Thou, which hast showed me great and sore troubles,
shalt quicken me again, and shalt bring me up again
from the depths of the earth.
Psalm 71:20

Holy Spirit

And I will pray the Father,
and he shall give you
another Comforter,
that he may abide
with you for ever;
Even the Spirit of truth;
whom the world
cannot receive,
because it seeth him not,
neither knoweth him:
but ye know him;
for he dwelleth with you,
and shall be in you.
John 14:16–17

Behold, I will pour out
my spirit unto you,
I will make known my words unto you.

Proverbs 1:23

He that believeth on me, as the scripture hath said,
out of his belly shall flow rivers of living water.
(But this spake he of the Spirit, which they that
believe on him should receive: for the Holy Ghost was not yet given;
because that Jesus was not yet glorified.)

John 7:38–39

Howbeit when he, the Spirit of truth, is come,
he will guide you into all truth: for he shall not speak of himself;
but whatsoever he shall hear, that shall he speak:
and he will show you things to come.

John 16:13

HONESTY

Are there yet the treasures of wickedness
in the house of the wicked,
and the scant measure that is abominable?
Shall I count them pure with the wicked balances,
and with the bag of deceitful weights?
For the rich men thereof are full of violence,
and the inhabitants thereof have spoken lies,
and their tongue is deceitful in their mouth.
Micah 6:10–12

Honesty

Ye shall not steal, neither deal falsely,
neither lie one to another.
Leviticus 19:11

Ye shall do no unrighteousness in judgment, in meteyard,
in weight, or in measure.
Leviticus 19:35

A false balance is abomination to the LORD:
but a just weight is his delight.
Proverbs 11:1

But thou shalt have a perfect and just weight,
a perfect and just measure shalt thou have: that thy days may
be lengthened in the land which the LORD thy God giveth thee.
For all that do such things, and all that do unrighteously,
are an abomination unto the LORD thy God.
Deuteronomy 25:15–16

Hope

Why art thou cast down, O my soul? and why art thou disquieted within me? hope thou in God: for I shall yet praise him, who is the health of my countenance, and my God.
Psalm 42:11

Who by him do believe in God, that raised him up from the dead, and gave him glory; that your faith and hope might be in God.
1 Peter 1:21

Wherefore gird up the loins of your mind, be sober,
and hope to the end for the grace that is to be brought unto you
at the revelation of Jesus Christ.
1 Peter 1:13

And every man that hath this hope in him purifieth himself, even as he is pure.
1 John 3:3

The wicked is driven away in his wickedness:
but the righteous hath hope in his death.
Proverbs 14:32

For the hope which is laid up for you in heaven,
whereof ye heard before in the word of the truth of the gospel. . .
Colossians 1:5

. . .Christ in you, the hope of glory.
Colossians 1:27

Be of good courage, and he shall strengthen your heart,
all ye that hope in the LORD.
Psalm 31:24

For thou art my hope, O Lord GOD:
thou art my trust from my youth.
Psalm 71:5

Blessed be the God and Father of our Lord Jesus Christ,
which according to his abundant mercy hath begotten us
again unto a lively hope
by the resurrection of Jesus Christ from the dead.
1 Peter 1:3

HOSPITALITY

Use hospitality one to another without grudging.
As every man hath received the gift, even so minister
the same one to another, as good stewards
of the manifold grace of God.
1 Peter 4:9–10

Hospitality

If a brother or sister be naked,
and destitute of daily food,
And one of you say unto them, Depart in peace,
be ye warmed and filled; notwithstanding
ye give them not those things which are needful to the body;
what doth it profit?
James 2:15–16

For whosoever shall give you a cup of water to drink in my name,
because ye belong to Christ, verily I say unto you,
he shall not lose his reward.
Mark 9:41

I have showed you all things, how that so labouring
ye ought to support the weak, and to remember the words of the Lord
Jesus, how he said, It is more blessed to give than to receive.
Acts 20:35

Humility

Whosoever therefore shall humble himself as this little child,
the same is greatest in the kingdom of heaven.
Matthew 18:4

Lord, thou hast heard the desire of the humble:
thou wilt prepare their heart, thou wilt cause thine ear to hear.
Psalm 10:17

And whosoever shall exalt himself shall be abased;
and he that shall humble himself shall be exalted.
Matthew 23:12

*When men are cast down, then thou shalt say,
There is lifting up;
and he shall save the humble person.*
Job 22:29

Better it is to be of an humble spirit with the lowly,
than to divide the spoil with the proud.
Proverbs 16:19

But he giveth more grace. Wherefore he saith,
God resisteth the proud, but giveth grace unto the humble.
James 4:6

Joy

For ye shall go out with joy,
and be led forth with peace:
the mountains and the hills
shall break forth
before you into singing,
and all the trees of the field
shall clap their hands.
Isaiah 55:12

Joy

Blessed is the people that know the joyful sound:
they shall walk, O LORD, in the light of thy countenance.
In thy name shall they rejoice all the day:
in thy righteousness shall they be exalted.
Psalm 89:15–16

The voice of rejoicing and salvation is in
the tabernacles of the righteous:
the right hand of the LORD doeth valiantly.
Psalm 118:15

Thou hast put gladness in my heart,
more than in the time that their corn and their wine increased.
Psalm 4:7

These things have I spoken unto you,
that my joy might remain in you, and that your joy might be full.
John 15:11

They that sow in tears shall reap in joy.
He that goeth forth and weepeth, bearing precious seed,
shall doubtless come again with rejoicing,
bringing his sheaves with him.
Psalm 126:5–6

For then shalt thou have thy delight in the Almighty, and shalt lift up thy face unto God.
Job 22:26

Light is sown for the righteous, and gladness
for the upright in heart. Rejoice in the LORD, ye righteous;
and give thanks at the remembrance of his holiness.
Psalm 97:11–12

Yet I will rejoice in the LORD, I will joy in the God of my salvation.
Habakkuk 3:18

LONELINESS

I will not leave you comfortless:
I will come to you.
John 14:18

Then shalt thou call, and the
LORD shall answer;
thou shalt cry,
and he shall say, Here I am.
Isaiah 58:9

Loneliness

Since thou wast precious in my sight,
thou hast been honourable,
and I have loved thee.
Isaiah 43:4

I will receive you, and will be a Father unto you,
and ye shall be my sons and daughters, saith the Lord Almighty.
2 Corinthians 6:17–18

And, behold, I am with thee, and will keep thee in all places
whither thou goest, and will bring thee again into this land;
for I will not leave thee, until I have done
that which I have spoken to thee of.
Genesis 28:15

And ye are complete in him,
which is the the head of all principality and power.
Colossians 2:10

Long Life

And even to your old age I am he;
and even to hoar hairs will I carry you: I have made,
and I will bear; even I will carry, and will deliver you.
Isaiah 46:4

With the ancient is wisdom; and in length of days understanding.
With him is wisdom and strength, he hath counsel and understanding.
Job 12:12–13

The glory of young men is their strength:
and the beauty of old men is the grey head.
Proverbs 20:29

Children's children are the crown of old men;
and the glory of children are their fathers.
Proverbs 17:6

*Thou shalt come to thy grave in a full age,
like as a shock of corn cometh in in his season.*
Job 5:26

And thine age shall be clearer than the noonday;
thou shalt shine forth, thou shalt be as the morning.
Job 11:17

Brotherly Love

A new commandment
I give unto you,
That ye love one another;
as I have loved you,
that ye also love one another.
By this shall all men know
that ye are my disciples,
if ye have love one to another.
John 13:34–35

Let love be without dissimulation.
Abhor that which is evil; cleave to that which is good.
Be kindly affectioned one to another with brotherly love;
in honour preferring one another.
Romans 12:9–10

But as touching brotherly love ye need not that I write unto you:
for ye yourselves are taught of God to love one another.
1 Thessalonians 4:9

He that loveth his brother abideth in the light,
and there is none occasion of stumbling in him.
1 John 2:10

Seeing ye have purified your souls in obeying the truth
through the Spirit unto unfeigned love of the brethren,
see that ye love one another with a pure heart fervently.
1 Peter 1:22

God's Love

For God so loved the world, that he gave his only begotten Son,
that whosoever believeth in him should not perish,
but have everlasting life.
John 3:16

And he will love thee, and bless thee,
and multiply thee:
he will also bless the fruit of thy womb,
and the fruit of thy land,
thy corn, and thy wine, and thine oil,
the increase of thy kine,
and the flocks of thy sheep, in the land
which he sware unto thy fathers to give thee.
Deuteronomy 7:13

The LORD openeth the eyes of the blind: the LORD raiseth them that are bowed down: the LORD loveth the righteous.
Psalm 146:8

The way of the wicked is an abomination unto the LORD: but he loveth him that followeth after righteousness.
Proverbs 15:9

Loving God

Know therefore that the LORD thy God, he is God, the faithful God, which keepeth covenant and mercy with them that love him and keep his commandments to a thousand generations.
Deuteronomy 7:9

I love them that love me;
and those that seek me early shall find me.
Proverbs 8:17

He that hath my commandments, and keepeth them,
he it is that loveth me: and he that loveth me shall be loved of my
Father, and I will love him, and will manifest myself to him.
John 14:21

That I may cause those that love me to inherit substance;
and I will fill their treasures.
Proverbs 8:21

Delight thyself also in the LORD;
and he shall give thee the desires of thine heart.

Psalm 37:4

Because he hath set his love upon me, therefore will I deliver him:
I will set him on high, because he hath known my name.
Psalm 91:14

Meekness

Blessed are the meek:
for they shall inherit the earth.
Matthew 5:5

But with righteousness
shall he judge the poor,
and reprove with equity
for the meek of the earth.
Isaiah 11:4

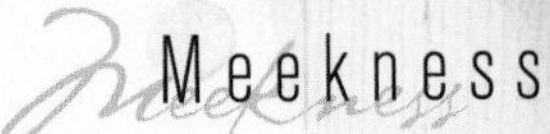

The meek also shall increase their joy in the LORD,
and the poor among men shall rejoice in the Holy One of Israel.
Isaiah 29:19

The LORD lifteth up the meek:
he casteth the wicked down to the ground.

Psalm 147:6

The meek will he guide in judgment:
and the meek will he teach his way.
Psalm 25:9

But the meek shall inherit the earth;
and shall delight themselves in the abundance of peace.
Psalm 37:11

MERCY

And therefore will the LORD wait, that he may be gracious unto you, and therefore will he be exalted, that he may have mercy upon you: for the LORD is a God of judgment: blessed are all they that wait for him.
Isaiah 30:18

Know therefore that God exacteth
of thee less than thine iniquity deserveth.
Job 11:6

Like as a father pitieth his children,
so the LORD pitieth them that fear him.
Psalm 103:13

But the mercy of the LORD is from everlasting to everlasting
upon them that fear him, and his righteousness unto children's children.
Psalm 103:17

And he said, I will make all my goodness pass before thee,
and I will proclaim the name of the LORD before thee;
and will be gracious to whom I will be gracious,
and will show mercy on whom I will show mercy.
Exodus 33:19

And I will have mercy upon her that had not obtained mercy;
and I will say to them which were not my people,
Thou art my people; and they shall say, Thou art my God.
Hosea 2:23

Obedience

See, I have set before thee
this day life and good, and death and evil;
In that I command thee
this day to love the Lord thy God,
to walk in his ways,
and to keep his commandments
and his statutes and his judgments,
that thou mayest live and multiply:
and the Lord thy God shall
bless thee in the land
whither thou goest to possess it.

Deuteronomy 30:15–16

And thou shalt do that which is right and good in the sight of the LORD: that it may be well with thee, and that thou mayest go in and possess the good land which the LORD sware unto thy fathers.
Deuteronomy 6:18

Hear therefore, O Israel, and observe to do it;
that it may be well with thee,
and that ye may increase mightily,
as the LORD God of thy fathers hath promised thee,
in the land that floweth
with milk and honey.
Deuteronomy 6:3

Wherefore it shall come to pass, if ye hearken to these judgments, and keep, and do them, that the LORD thy God shall keep unto thee the covenant and the mercy which he sware unto thy fathers.
Deuteronomy 7:12

PATIENCE

Be patient therefore, brethren, unto the coming
of the Lord. Behold, the husbandman waiteth for the precious fruit
of the earth, and hath long patience for it, until he receive the early
and latter rain. Be ye also patient; stablish
your hearts: for the coming of the Lord draweth nigh.
James 5:7–8

For what glory is it, if, when ye be buffeted for your faults,
ye shall take it patiently? but if, when ye do well, and suffer for it,
ye take it patiently, this is acceptable with God.
1 Peter 2:20

*And let us not be weary in well doing:
for in due season we shall reap, if we faint not.*
Galatians 6:9

Let us hold fast the profession of our faith without wavering;
(for he is faithful that promised).
Hebrews 10:23

But he that shall endure unto the end, the same shall be saved.
Matthew 24:13

PEACE

Peace, peace to him
that is far off,
and to him that is near,
saith the LORD;
and I will heal him.
Isaiah 57:19

And let the peace
of God rule in your hearts,
to the which also
ye are called in one body;
and be ye thankful.
Colossians 3:15

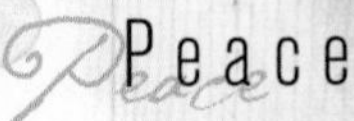

I will hear what God the LORD will speak:
for he will speak peace unto his people, and to his saints.
Psalm 85:8

And the peace of God, which passeth all understanding,
shall keep your hearts and minds through Christ Jesus.
Philippians 4:7

And the work of righteousness shall be peace;
and the effect of righteousness quietness and assurance for ever.
Isaiah 32:17

*Mark the perfect man, and behold the upright:
for the end of that man is peace.*
Psalm 37:37

PRAYER

Ask, and it shall be given you; seek, and ye shall find;
knock, and it shall be opened unto you:
For every one that asketh receiveth; and he that seeketh findeth;
and to him that knocketh it shall be opened.
Matthew 7:7–8

And all things, whatsoever ye shall ask in prayer, believing, ye shall receive.

Matthew 21:22

He will be very gracious unto thee at the voice of thy cry;
when he shall hear it, he will answer thee.
Isaiah 30:19

And this is the confidence that we have in him,
that, if we ask any thing according to his will, he heareth us:
And if we know that he hear us, whatsoever we ask,
we know that we have the petitions that we desired of him.
1 John 5:14–15

And it shall come to pass, that before they call,
I will answer; and while they are yet speaking, I will hear.
Isaiah 65:24

Whatsoever ye shall ask the Father in my name,
he will give it you. Hitherto have ye asked nothing in my name:
ask, and ye shall receive, that your joy may be full.
John 16:23–24

Confess your faults one to another, and pray one for another,
that ye may be healed. The effectual fervent prayer
of a righteous man availeth much.
James 5:16

*Thou shalt make thy prayer unto him,
and he shall hear thee.*
Job 22:27

And whatsoever ye shall ask in my name,
that will I do, that the Father may be glorified in the Son.
If ye shall ask any thing in my name, I will do it.
John 14:13–14

If ye abide in me, and my words abide in you,
ye shall ask what ye will, and it shall be done unto you.
John 15:7

God's Protection

The name of the Lord is a strong tower:
the righteous runneth into it, and is safe.
Proverbs 18:10

At destruction and famine thou shalt laugh:
neither shalt thou be afraid of the beasts of the earth.
Job 5:22

God's Protection

And thou shalt be secure, because there is hope; yea,
thou shalt dig about thee, and thou shalt take thy rest in safety.
Also thou shalt lie down, and none shall make thee afraid;
yea, many shall make suit unto thee.
Job 11:18–19

The LORD shall preserve thee from all evil: he shall preserve thy soul.
The LORD shall preserve thy going out and thy coming
in from this time forth, and even for evermore.
Psalm 121:7–8

When thou liest down, thou shalt not be afraid:
yea, thou shalt lie down, and thy sleep shall be sweet.
Proverbs 3:24

And who is he that will harm you,
if ye be followers of that which is good?
1 Peter 3:13

Repentance

The time is fulfilled,
and the kingdom of God is at hand:
repent ye, and believe the gospel.
Mark 1:15

And they went out,
and preached that men should repent.
Mark 6:12

The LORD is nigh unto them that are of a broken heart;
and saveth such as be of a contrite spirit.
Psalm 34:18

He healeth the broken in heart,
and bindeth up their wounds.
Psalm 147:3

If iniquity be in thine hand, put it far away,
and let not wickedness dwell in thy tabernacles.
For then shalt thou lift up thy face without spot;
yea, thou shalt be stedfast, and shalt not fear.
Job 11:14–15

For I am not come to call the righteous,
but sinners to repentance.
Matthew 9:13

RIGHTEOUSNESS

For the LORD God is a sun and shield:
the LORD will give grace and glory:
no good thing will he withhold
from them that walk uprightly.
Psalm 84:11

The young lions do lack, and suffer hunger:
but they that seek the LORD shall not want any good thing.
Psalm 34:10

The fear of the wicked, it shall come upon him:
but the desire of the righteous shall be granted.
Proverbs 10:24

Evil pursueth sinners:
but to the righteous good shall be repayed.
Proverbs 13:21

A good man obtaineth
favour of the LORD:
but a man of wicked
devices will he condemn.

Proverbs 12:2

But seek ye first the kingdom of God,
and his righteousness;
and all these things
shall be added unto you.
Matthew 6:33

SALVATION

Therefore if any man be in Christ,
he is a new creature:
old things are passed away;
behold, all things
are become new.
2 Corinthians 5:17

For he hath made him to be sin
for us, who knew no sin;
that we might be made
the righteousness of God in him.
2 Corinthians 5:21

Salvation

Jesus answered and said unto him, Verily, verily, I say unto thee,
Except a man be born again, he cannot see the kingdom of God.
Nicodemus saith unto him, How can a man be born when he is old?
can he enter the second time into his mother's womb, and be born?
Jesus answered, Verily, verily, I say unto thee, Except a man be born
of water and of the Spirit, he cannot enter into the kingdom of God.
That which is born of the flesh is flesh; and that
which is born of the Spirit is spirit.
Marvel not that I said unto thee, Ye must be born again.
John 3:3–7

And you hath he quickened, who were dead in trespasses and sins.
Ephesians 2:1

For this is good and acceptable in the sight of God our Saviour;
Who will have all men to be saved, and to come
unto the knowledge of the truth.
1 Timothy 2:3–4

SEEKING GOD

The LORD is with you, while ye be with him; and if ye seek him, he will be found of you; but if ye forsake him, he will forsake you.
2 Chronicles 15:2

Sow to yourselves in righteousness, reap in mercy; break up your fallow ground: for it is time to seek the LORD, till he come and rain righteousness upon you.
Hosea 10:12

But without faith it is impossible to please him:
for he that cometh to God must believe that he is,
and that he is a rewarder of them that diligently seek him.
Hebrews 11:6

That they should seek the Lord, if haply they might feel after him,
and find him, though he be not far from every one of us.
Acts 17:27

*The LORD is good unto them that wait for him,
to the soul that seeketh him.*

Lamentations 3:25

But if from thence thou shalt seek the LORD thy God, thou shalt find him,
if thou seek him with all thy heart and with all thy soul.
Deuteronomy 4:29

REDEMPTION FROM SIN

And she shall bring forth a son,
and thou shalt call his name
JESUS: for he shall save his people
from their sins.
Matthew 1:21

Be it known unto you therefore,
men and brethren, that through
this man is preached
unto you the forgiveness of sins.
Acts 13:38

Redemption from Sin

Who gave himself for our sins, that he might deliver us
from this present evil world,
according to the will of God and our Father.
Galatians 1:4

And if any man sin, we have an advocate with the Father, Jesus Christ the righteous: And he is the propitiation for our sins: and not for ours only, but also for the sins of the whole world.
1 John 2:1–2

Who his own self bare our sins in his own body on the tree,
that we, being dead to sins, should live unto righteousness:
by whose stripes ye were healed.
1 Peter 2:24

This is a faithful saying, and worthy of all acceptation, that Christ Jesus came into the world to save sinners; of whom I am chief.
1 Timothy 1:15

TRUST

God is our refuge and strength,
a very present help in trouble.
Therefore will not we fear,
though the earth be removed,
and though the mountains
be carried into
the midst of the sea.
Psalm 46:1–2

Trust

For the LORD God is a sun and shield:
the LORD will give grace and glory:
no good thing will he withhold from them that walk uprightly.
O LORD of hosts, blessed is the man that trusteth in thee.
Psalm 84:11–12

Trust in the LORD, and do good; so shalt thou dwell in the land,
and verily thou shalt be fed.
Delight thyself also in the LORD;
and he shall give thee the desires of thine heart.
Commit thy way unto the LORD; trust also in him;
and he shall bring it to pass.
Psalm 37:3–5

Trust in the LORD with all thine heart;
and lean not unto thine own understanding.
In all thy ways acknowledge him, and he shall direct thy paths.
Proverbs 3:5–6

Fear not, little flock; for it is your Father's
good pleasure to give you the kingdom.
Luke 12:32

Casting all your care upon him;
for he careth for you.
1 Peter 5:7

They that trust in the LORD shall be as mount Zion,
which cannot be removed, but abideth for ever.
Psalm 125:1

Therefore take no thought, saying, What shall we eat? or,
What shall we drink? or, Wherewithal shall we be clothed?
(For after all these things do the Gentiles seek:)
for your heavenly Father knoweth that ye have need of all these things.
Matthew 6:31–32

WISDOM

If any of you lack wisdom, let him ask of God,
that giveth to all men liberally, and upbraideth not;
and it shall be given him.
James 1:5

And he will teach us of his ways, and we will walk in his paths.
Isaiah 2:3

I will instruct thee and teach thee in the way which thou shalt go:
I will guide thee with mine eye.
Psalm 32:8

For God giveth to a man that is good in his sight wisdom,
and knowledge, and joy.
Ecclesiastes 2:26

I will bless the LORD, who hath given me counsel:
my reins also instruct me in the night seasons.
Psalm 16:7

Then shalt thou understand the fear of the LORD,
and find the knowledge of God. For the LORD giveth wisdom:
out of his mouth cometh knowledge and understanding.
He layeth up sound wisdom for righteous:
he is a buckler to them that walk uprightly.
Proverbs 2:5–7

Word of God

For I am not ashamed of the gospel of Christ:
for it is the power of God unto salvation
to every one that believeth.
Romans 1:16

Blessed is he that readeth, and they
that hear the words of this prophecy,
and keep those things which are written therein:
for the time is at hand.
Revelation 1:3

We have also a more sure word of prophecy;
whereunto ye do well that ye take heed, as unto a light
that shineth in a dark place, until the day dawn,
and the day star arise in your hearts.
2 Peter 1:19

For the word of God is quick, and powerful, and sharper
than any twoedged sword, piercing even to the dividing asunder
of soul and spirit, and of the joints and marrow, and is a discerner
of the thoughts and intents of the heart.
Hebrews 4:12

Worry

Be careful for nothing;
but in every thing by prayer and supplication
with thanksgiving let your requests
be made known unto God.
And the peace of God,
which passeth all understanding,
shall keep your hearts
and minds through Christ Jesus.

Philippians 4:6–7

God is our refuge and strength, a very present help in trouble.
Therefore will not we fear, though the earth be removed, and though the mountains be carried into the midst of the sea;
Though the waters thereof roar and be troubled, though the mountains shake with the swelling thereof.
Psalm 46:1–3

For he shall be as a tree planted by the waters,
and that spreadeth out her roots by the river,
and shall not see when heat cometh, but her leaf shall be green;
and shall not be careful in the year of drought,
neither shall cease from yielding fruit.
Jeremiah 17:8

And Jesus answered and said unto her, Martha, Martha,
thou art careful and troubled about many things:
But one thing is needful: and Mary hath chosen that good part,
which shall not be taken away from her.
Luke 10:41–42

WORSHIP

All the earth shall worship thee,
and shall sing unto thee;
they shall sing to thy name.
Psalm 66:4

O come, let us worship
and bow down:
let us kneel before the LORD
our maker.
For he is our God;
and we are the people
of his pasture,
and the sheep of his hand.
Psalm 95:6–7

Exalt the LORD our God, and worship at his holy hill;
for the LORD our God is holy.
Psalm 99:9

Now when Jesus was born in Bethlehem of Judaea in the days of Herod the king, behold, there came wise men from the east to Jerusalem, Saying, Where is he that is born King of the Jews? for we have seen his star in the east, and are come to worship him.
Matthew 2:1–2

God is a Spirit: and they that worship him must worship him in spirit and in truth.
John 4:24

All nations whom thou hast made shall come and worship before thee, O Lord; and shall glorify thy name.
Psalm 86:9

Track	Title	Time	© ℗
1	Be Still/How Precious, O Lord	6:23	(1)
2	The Gospel Was Written	3:13	(2)
3	My God Will Supply	3:10	(2)
4	I Believe There Is a God in Heaven	2:52	(1)
5	Make Us One, Lord	3:44	(2)
6	Fear Not	2:55	(2)
7	Let There Be Love	2:36	(1)
8	Sing a New Song to Him	2:14	(2)
9	He Shall Comfort the Earth	3:24	(2)
10	All Heaven Declares	2:41	(1)

TOTAL RUNNING TIME (33:18)